"It's very interesting," said Alice, after she had finished,
"but I don't quite understand it."
"You will absorb it after awhile," said the frog, as he got
up and walked away, "if you have the faculty."

R.C. EVARTS'S

Alice's Adventures in ~~Wonderland~~ *Cambridge*

ILLUSTRATED BY E.L. BARON

with a new foreword by
THE HARVARD LAMPOON

Charleston  London

THE
History
PRESS

Published by The History Press
Charleston, SC 29403
www.historypress.net

Originally published by the Cambridge University Press, 1913
The History Press edition 2008

Manufactured in the United States

ISBN 978.1.59629.605.3

Library of Congress Cataloging-in-Publication Data
Evarts, R. C. (Richard Conover), b. 1890.
  Alice's adventures in Cambridge / R.C. Evarts ; illustrated by E.L. Barron ; with a
new foreword by The Harvard Lampoon.
     p. cm.
  ISBN 978-1-59629-605-3
  1. Harvard University--Humor. 2. College students--Massachusetts--Cambridge--
Humor. 3. College wit and humor. I. Carroll, Lewis, 1832-1898. Alice's adventures
in wonderland. II. Harvard lampoon. III. Title.
  LD2153.9.E8 2008
  378.19'8--dc22
                              2008040905

From the Publisher:

This new edition contains the full text from the original 1913 edition, published by the Cambridge University Press, Cambridge, Massachusetts. All efforts have been made to maintain the integrity of the original work, including spelling, dialect and punctuation.

Our thanks to Gus Sousa, rare book collector from Salem, Massachusetts, for bringing the original *Harvard Lampoon* house copy of *Alice* to our attention.

Contents

Editors' Note

For those of us like the Dormouse who are "neither athletic nor prominent," stumbling into "the Yard" can be about as bewildering as falling into a rabbit hole. When narrated by the legendary *Harvard Lampoon*, the trip is all the more—well—trippy. Nearly a century after its first publication, we think *Alice's Adventures in Cambridge* is still a delight. And though we, like you no doubt, had to look up allusions to purple socks, Keezer's Clothing and the Manter Hall School, the peculiarities of prestige and the allure of elitism remain timeless.

– The Editors of The History Press

FOREWORD

Often, we intentionally schedule writers meetings on Friday and Saturday nights, just so we'll have an excuse to hang out at the Lampoon Castle. People will come in and pretend to be really mad but will stay for the entire night. Usually, all forty members of staff attend these meetings, as well as several graduates and trustees. So when we first heard about the opportunity to write this introduction, everyone on staff got really excited. For at least a couple Fridays and Saturdays, we had a legitimate reason to be sitting around talking about comedy all night.

Since its founding in 1876, the *Lampoon* has been known on a national scale for two things: pranks and parodies. While everyone knows about the time we stole Burt Ward's "Robin" costume, or the time we smeared meat sauce on the walls of a library and then released several rabid dogs, or all the times we tricked Harvard into not suspending us, there are a couple lesser-known pranks that might shed some light on our comedic sensibilities and also help us hit our publisher's minimum word count.

In 1945, *Lampoon* members got their hands on the key to J. Robert Oppenheimer's Los Alamos laboratory. They broke in and stole the atomic bomb, only to return it hours later with ketchup all over the handles. In 1969, *Lampoon* members kidnapped the commissioner of the National Basketball Association (NBA) right before the draft and hired an impersonator to go out and announce the picks *with his fly completely open*. More recently, the entire *Lampoon* attended the Indianapolis 500 carrying hundreds of banana peels. Twenty minutes before the race, staff members found their way to the track and, after slashing Wally Dalenbach Sr.'s tires, kidnapped him and forced him to sit in a room full of banana peels, to which he was moderately allergic.

But we also do parodies. Over the years, the *Lampoon* has produced countless parodies in a variety of forms. Past victims include: *Literary Digest* (1925), *Newsweek* (1947 and 1956), *Playboy* (1966), the *New York Times* (1968), *Cosmopolitan* (1972), *People* (1981), *Entertainment Weekly* (1994) and, most recently, *National Geographic* (2008). We've also been trying to release a *Catcher in the Rye* parody, but each year we forget to mail in the final draft. Someone keeps saying he's going to do it, but ultimately forgets or gets too drunk to remember where he put it. This has happened every year since 1967.

The process of writing a parody is equal parts exciting and exhausting. Usually after writing a parody, we'll all go into comas for at least half a year. We begin the process by meeting in the writers' room. There, we argue whether or not we should order pizza for the meeting. This can take upwards of four hours. Once we come up with an idea for a parody, we start writing on our mainframe computer. Whenever we're coming up with jokes for a parody, no matter how good or bad they are, we never press delete. I guess this rule exists because it's good to get all our ideas out, though it could be because the delete key has soy sauce under it and always causes the system to crash. If we ever run dry of jokes, we summon joke specialist Barry Mendelbaum for $4.99/joke.

One of the most important steps in writing a parody is tricking the person/people whose work you're parodying into throwing you a lavish launch party complete with hors d'oeuvres and wine tables that don't ask for identification. Sometimes, publications will throw you multiple parties. For example, when we parodied *Mademoiselle* in 1961, they threw us a pre-launch party, a mid-launch party, a post-launch party and a celebratory lunch.

But the best part of the process is, as it should be, the final product. The work you're reading right now is especially exciting because it parodies the work of Lewis Carroll, a thoroughly fascinating author and thinker. His most famous book was published in 1865. The current title—*Alice's Adventures in Wonderland*—came after a long debate with publishers, during which several other titles—including *Alice Among the Fairies*, *Alice's Golden Hour* and *The Great Gatsby*—were considered but ultimately abandoned. It is also worth noting that Carroll went on to write and publish a sequel, entitled *Through the Looking-Glass*. In both of these works, it is unconfirmed whether or not he wrote parts under the influence of drugs, even though his work has psychedelic undertones and remnants of opium were found in his desk drawer.

Our parody, *Alice's Adventures in Cambridge*, is little read by today's general population, who have consigned it—on account of its numerous obscure allusions and time-sensitive references—to the realm of incomprehensibility. Nevertheless, this forgotten little tome, the book that *Lampoon* founder John Tyler Wheelwright legendarily called "my cute little bastard" (in a nod to its origin among unmarried writers), has attained, through the decades, something of the status of a "cult hit" among *Lampoon* staffers. We consider it to be, if not our "best" parody, then certainly our most inaccessible. Not that this should stop the well-intentioned naïve reader from making an attempt, or giving up actual money for the chance to do so.

In a testament to its relevance (for us, at least), *Alice* has entered our lexicon. Members of the *Lampoon* don't "write" comedy, we "alice" it. We don't go on outings, we go on "adventures"— Alice's. We don't "attend" classes at Harvard, we "alice" them, which means to "not attend." When we pass each other in the numerous labyrinthine tunnels beneath our building, we don't greet each other verbally, but instead we nod silently, mouthing "alice."

But these influences, which the casual reader might call superficial and irrelevant, are only the very beginning of a massive accumulation of superficiality and irrelevance. *Alice* is everywhere at the *Lampoon*, and not just because we ritually burn copies and spread the ashes throughout our building. You would be hard pressed to find a member of the *Lampoon* who doesn't think about it for at least ten seconds every day, perhaps in between his daily exercise regimen and his third meal, both of which we call "alice-mas." Needless to say, we consider this parody to be an important part of the *Lampoon* soul, and we hope that once you have read it, you will too.

This old book is so dear to our hearts that it holds a special place in the *Lampoon* library, a century-old collection housed inside our building that comprises literally millions of molecules. In order to understand precisely how special is the place that this book occupies, one would need to study the intricacies of our system of classification, which has been scientifically proven to be over a thousand times more convoluted than the Dewey decimal system. But if you must know, we keep it under "parodies."

It's hard to imagine 1913, the year *Alice* was released to endless acclaim. People were counting the days since the still freshly remembered

Titanic disaster, and counting *down* the days until World War I. President Taft was gearing up for his reelection campaign against the Bull Moose Roosevelt and newcomer Wilson, and women everywhere were burning their husbands' breakfasts in anxious anticipation of getting the right to vote. It is within this complex historical context that we must attempt to understand *Alice*, before we give up, realizing that it makes literally no sense.

Once released, so many copies of the parody were ordered that a second printing was needed at once. No other book was cheaper, and *Alice*, with its inflammable pages, is partly credited for helping the grateful citizens of Cambridge get through the roughest winter in decades. If that is its sole achievement—as is almost certainly the case—then we can be satisfied that *Alice* made a difference. Thank you for purchasing your copy: with oil prices what they are, it is no surprise that you did.

The Harvard Lampoon
August 2008

INTRODUCTION

In all fiction there is no character that delights the hearts of both young and old more than Alice. The collaborators in this small book cast their product on a cold unfeeling world with the utmost apologies to Lewis Caroll and John Tenniel; and with an ill-nourished hope that those who read will do so with a lenient eye. The idea was conceived of transplanting Alice to Cambridge, and there showing her some of the strange things that may be found in that peculiar place. She found many curious creatures and had many wonderful Adventures.

These few chapters appeared first in the "Harvard Lampoon"—that Prince of humorous papers. They have now collected themselves, and here stand ready to meet the fierce glare of publicity.

Cambridge, Mass., June 17, 1913.

Chapter I

THE INFECTION MEETING

Alice was just about to enter one of the tempting little shops with purple socks and ties in the window, when she saw the White Rabbit hurrying across a mud puddle. She ran after him, and caught him just as he reached a curbstone.

"Please—" she began.

But the White Rabbit did not even turn his head.

"No, I haven't any pennies," he said.

"But I wanted to know—" said Alice.

"Oh, it's you, is it?" the White Rabbit said, turning round and blowing a huge cloud of smoke from his pipe into Alice's face. "Well, come on."

"Where?" asked Alice.

"To the Infection Meeting, of course," said the White Rabbit, starting off at a rapid pace.

"But I don't want to be infected," Alice said, as she ran after him. "I've had the mumps once, and the measles, and ever so many other things."

"Ah! But you haven't had probation yet," said the White Rabbit, "and you'll catch it sure if you don't go to your Infection Meetings. I'm a Sophomore and I ought to know. Come on."

"Who will give it to me?" asked Alice, feeling a little alarmed.

"The Queen, of course. Come on."

Alice didn't like being ordered about in this way, but she followed the White Rabbit, who led her to a room filled with animals of all kinds sitting on benches. At one end of the room was a platform where a large frog sat behind a desk. He was a very young-looking frog, Alice thought, but he looked so severe that she sat down quietly beside the White Rabbit.

The frog, after looking more severe than ever, suddenly began to write very fast on a blackboard behind him. Alice tried to make

out what he was writing, but it seemed to be chiefly nonsense. It ran something like this:

"If, other things being equal, the level of prices should rise, and thus falling create a demand and supply with, and as which, would you consider this a division of labor? If so, when, and in what capacity? If not, why not, and under what circumstances?"

As soon as he had finished, all the other animals produced paper from nowhere in particular, and began to scribble as fast as they could. Alice noticed that the Lizard, who was sitting in the front row, was the only one who wrote anything original. All the others copied from his paper, and crowded round him so closely that Alice was afraid the poor little creature would be smothered. Meanwhile the frog looked at the ceiling. "He couldn't look anywhere else, poor thing," thought Alice; "his eyes are in the top of his head."

About two seconds had passed when the frog called out "Time!" and began to gather up the papers. When he had collected them all, he took them to his desk and began to mark them.

He marked the first one A, the second one B, and so on down to F, when he began over again with A. All this time he kept his eyes tight shut. "So he will be sure to be impartial," the White Rabbit explained to Alice.

After the marking was finished, the frog handed the papers back to their owners. The White Rabbit, who had written nothing at all, had a large A on his paper. The Lizard, however, had an F marked on his.

"A," said the White Rabbit to Alice, "means that I wrote an excellent paper."

"But you wrote nothing," objected Alice.

"Nothing succeeds like success," said the White Rabbit, and hurried away, leaving Alice a little puzzled.

Meanwhile all the animals except the frog had disappeared.

"Would you mind telling me," began Alice, feeling that there ought to be some conversation, "why you—"

"Certainly not," said the frog, handing her a book. "I think you will find this a very able exposition of the subject."

Alice opened the book, and finding it to be poetry, she read the first piece through.

Jabberwocky

'Twas taussig, and the bushnell hart
Did byron hurlbut in the rand,
All barrett was the wendell (Bart.)
*And the charles t. cope-*land.

Beware the Münsterberg, my son!
'Twill read your mind—you bet it can!
Beware the Grandgent bird, and shun
The frisky Merriman.

He took his bursar sword in hand:
Long time his neilson foe he sought—
So rested he by the bernbaum tree,
And stood awhile in thought.

And as in coolidge thought he stood,
The Münsterberg, with eyes of flame,
Came spalding through the perry wood,
And babbit as it came!

One, two! One, two! And through and through
The bursar blade went snicker-snack!
He left it dead, and with its head
He santayanad back.

And hast thou slain the Münsterberg?
Come to my arms, my bierwirth boy!
O Kittredge day! Allard! Bôcher!
He schofield in his joy.

'Twas taussig, and the bushnell hart
Did byron hurlbut in the rand,
All barrett was the wendell (Bart.)
*And the charles t. cope-*land.

"It's very interesting," said Alice, after she had finished, "but I don't *quite* understand it."

"You will absorb it after awhile," said the frog, as he got up and walked away, "if you have the faculty."

Chapter II
HUMPTY DUMPTY OF MANTER HALL

After carefully stepping over all the mud-puddles, Alice at last reached the sidewalk, and to her astonishment saw a large cat bowing and smiling before her.

"Good morning, sir," said the cat, "anything for Max to-day?"

"I didn't know cats could talk!" cried Alice in surprise.

"I'm a Keezer Cat. All Keezer cats can talk," replied the cat, grinning more than ever; "anything for Max to-day?"

"Who is Max, and what does he want?" Alice asked.

"This is Max," said the cat, and disappeared with a bow.

Alice walked on another block, and was about to turn down a side street, when she was startled by a voice saying, "Anything for Max to-day?" and, turning round, saw the Keezer Cat at her elbow.

"Goodness!" cried Alice, "I wish you wouldn't frighten one so. You almost made me jump out of my skin."

"I wish you *would* jump out of your skin," the Keezer Cat replied, "then I'd buy it from you. After you had jumped out you wouldn't need it any more, you know."

"But I don't want to sell my skin," said Alice. "It's too useful."

"I'll give you fifty cents for it," the cat said, "and be robbing myself at that."

Alice paid no attention to this remark. She thought it sounded bloodthirsty, and, feeling a little afraid of being skinned alive, she hurried on. When she came to the next corner, there was the cat again, grinning as much as ever.

"Come, I'll match you whether I pay you a dollar or nothing," said the cat, edging up very close.

"How do you happen to be on *every* corner?" Alice asked, hoping to change the subject.

"I live on street corners," replied the cat, "and I'll give you seventy-five cents for your skin, on the spot. It would ruin me to go any higher."

The insistence of the animal frightened Alice so much that she began to run. After she had run what seemed at least three miles, and jumped over about a thousand puddles, and overtaken and passed eighteen street-cars, she came to a stop in front of one of the strangest looking objects she had ever seen. It looked very much like an egg, and yet it certainly was a person, for it had eyes, nose, and mouth, and even a moustache. It was seated on a high board fence on which was a sign with "NO PASSING THROUGH" on it in large letters.

"You can't pass," cried the creature as Alice approached; "that is, unless I allow you to. Nobody can pass without my help."

"Whom have I the honor of addressing?" asked Alice.

"Humpty Dumpty of Manter Hall," said the creature, extending his hand. "How do you do?"

Alice could not help repeating to herself the old nursery rhyme:

"Humpty Dumpty of Manter Hall,
If it weren't for you we'd go to the wall,
All the Dean's office and all the Dean's men
Would be forced to double their business then."

"Are you coming to my Seminar?" asked Humpty Dumpty after a pause. "A Seminar is a place where you can learn in three hours what it takes a Professor three months to teach."

"How very convenient," Alice said. "Could you explain something now for me?"

"I already know what you are going to ask," said Humpty Dumpty. "From long practice in foretelling examination questions I have become a regular clairvoyant. You were about to ask me why I am a Widow. Because men may come, and men may go, but I go on forever, of course. That's too easy. Ask another."

"But that isn't my question at all," said Alice. "I just wanted you to explain some poetry I read this morning. This is how it went:

"'Twas taussig, and the bushnell hart
Did byron hurlbut in the rand,
All barrett was the wendell (Bart.)
*And the charles t. cope-*land.*"*

"Nothing is easier," Humpty Dumpty replied. "Taussig means gusty, showery weather. A bushnell hart is an animal—a cross between a Bull Moose and a walrus. It has bushy hair, and lives on its reputation. To byron hurlbut is to pounce on people and worry them unreasonably. A rand is a classical place, unknown to many, and situated somewhere in the Sabbatical. Barrett is an adjective used to denote any member of the Royal Family of England. A wendell is a comparatively literary rarity indigenous to the English court. Bart. is English for Baronet. A charles t. is a kind of cherub which lives on cheap cigarettes and strange customs. It can be brought to bay in

its lair any time during the morning. Copeland is the past participle of a verb meaning to fly about in eccentric circles. Is there anything else I can tell you?"

"No, thank you," said Alice, "you are very kind, I am sure."

"Now you owe me thirty dollars," Humpty Dumpty said. "You had better make out a check."

"Dear me," said Alice to herself, "I never saw such mercenary creatures in my life."

Then a bright idea came into her head.

"Would you mind making out an itemized bill?" she asked.

"Certainly not," Humpty Dumpty replied, and taking out a large fountain-pen, began to write. While he busied himself thus, Alice slipped away, and was soon lost to sight among the red oak saplings.

Chapter III

THE MAD MEETING

After running a little way through the woods, Alice stopped in surprise before a table which was set out under a tree. The table was laid for at least thirty people, but only three were sitting at it. Alice immediately recognized the Hatter and the March Hare, and the third she was quite sure must be the Dormouse, as it was fast asleep. The Hatter wore a very high hat covered with eight or ten hatbands of various colors. As soon as he saw Alice he cried out, "Radcliffe not admitted!"

"But my name isn't Radcliffe," said Alice, as she took a seat.

"Nobody said it was," the Hatter replied.

"But you *looked* at me," said Alice.

"That was unavoidable," said the March Hare. "Nobody looks at Radcliffe students for pleasure."

"I don't think much of Nobody's taste then," said the Dormouse, waking up.

"Come, come," cried the Hatter, bringing a huge mallet down on the table with a crash. "The meeting is called to order."

"This is a meeting of the Student Council," the March Hare explained to Alice, "and we are the Student Council. At least," he said pointing to the Dormouse, "*he* is the Student, and *we* are the Council."

"Phibetakappa, Phibetakappa, Phibetakappa," murmured the Dormouse sleepily, and was immediately silenced by the Hatter hitting him over the head with the mallet.

"That's his way of apologizing for being here," said the March Hare. "You see he's neither athletic nor prominent."

"I suppose you are both," said Alice politely.

"No, I'm only athletic," replied the March Hare. "He's really prominent though," he went on, pointing to the Hatter. "See all his hatbands."

"Yes," said the Hatter proudly. "You see, this style of hat allows me to wear them all at once."

"But I don't see the object," said Alice.

"The object is plain enough," the March Hare said; "it is right underneath the hat."

"Order!" shouted the Hatter. "There is a motion before the house. All those in favor say aye. The ayes have it. The motion is carried."

"What was the motion?" asked Alice.

"I haven't the slightest idea," said the Hatter.

"Then I don't see how you can carry it, if you don't know what it is," said Alice rather impatiently.

"I didn't carry it. I passed it," the Hatter replied.

"But that's the same thing," said Alice.

"Not the same thing at all," said the March Hare. "You might as well say that a forward pass is the same thing as a touchdown."

"You might as well say," the Dormouse drowsily murmured, "that to pass with an A is the same thing as to fail with an E."

"You might as well say that the *Crime* is the same thing as the penalty," said the Hatter.

"It *is* the same thing, if you read it," said the March Hare.

Alice was silent. She felt somehow that they were all talking nonsense.

"Now," said the Hatter, after a pause, "we will turn to the very important question whether straw hats should be worn by the Student Body before the first of April."

"Is that as important as to decide who should be manager of the Chess Team?" asked the March Hare.

"Well," said the Hatter judicially, "it certainly ought to come before the question of Freshman nominations."

"Phibetakappa, Phibetakappa, Phibetakappa," the Dormouse began, and would have gone on indefinitely had not the March Hare shoved under its nose a large volume on Political Economy which so absorbed the little

animal that he subsided, and was soon asleep again.

"I don't see why you call this the Student Council," said Alice. "The Student part of it doesn't have any say at all."

"He can say only one thing, and it gets tiresome after a while," the Hatter answered. "Would you like to hear a song?"

"I should love to," said Alice, only too glad to keep out of an argument.

Thereupon the Hatter stood up, and began to sing, in a tune which was a mixture of "Fair Harvard," and "Yankee Doodle,"—

"We are the Student Council.
We were fathered by a Crime.
Our word is law,
Our law is words,
Believe me, every time.
We draw up constitutions,
We sub*mit resolutions,*
We cogitate,
We mediate,

We elevate,
We meditate,
And are known for doing nothing
In every land and clime."

"That's very pretty," said Alice. "I don't think I ever heard anything like it before."

"I hear you are on probation," said the March Hare looking severely at Alice. "Hereafter you can take part in no College Activities—By-law 68, Article 507, Section 1654 of the Revised Constitution."

This was so rude that it was beyond endurance. Alice got up and left without another word. As she walked away, she heard the Hatter and March Hare discussing violently whether the Student Body could wear a straw hat at all unless it had a head.

Chapter IV
ALICE MEETS THE BLACK KNIGHT AND THE CHANNING MOUSE

Alice gave a little scream of delight when she came in sight of Harvard Square.

"*Now* I know where I am," she said to herself. "I can tell by that—that—well, that big round thing in the middle. I declare! I do believe I have forgotten its name," she went on. "I wonder if I can remember my own. Let's see—is it Mabel? No. It must be Bertha. No, that's not right either. I know it began with an L. Oh dear, I really *have* forgotten it. What *shall* I do!"

Here Alice began to cry. You must remember she was a very little girl, and had never forgotten her name before.

"Come, come," said a voice, "don't cry. We have had enough rain lately."

"But I have forgotten my name," sobbed Alice.

"Oh, is that all?" said the voice. "Well, your name is Alice."

Alice looked up and saw the Black Knight standing in front of her. There was no mistaking him, because he wore a full suit of black tin armor.

"Thank you," said Alice. "I'm sure I don't know how I came to forget it."

"Is there anything else you would like to know?" said the Black Knight politely. "I can tell you your age, class, and marks for the last three years; also your brother's, father's, grandfather's and great-grandfather's names, classes, marks, and general appearance."

"What a wonderful person you must be!" said Alice, drying her eyes.

"Not at all," replied the Black Knight. "It is all in a day's work. You see, I have two assistants—the Queen and the Recorder."

"What does the Recorder do?" asked Alice.

"He counts the number of cuts it takes to sever connection with the University," the Black Knight answered.

"It must be very trying sort of work," said Alice.

"Yes, he's trying all the time," said the Black Knight, "but he never succeeds without the Queen's help."

"I suppose you know how to manage them," said Alice.

"Oh yes," the Black Knight said. "You see, they have to go to me for their facts. The fiction they do themselves. By the way, would you like to see an Iconoclast?"

"What is it?" asked Alice, not quite sure whether it was an animal or a Greek temple.

"Come on," said the Black Knight. "I'll show you."

Alice was doubtful at first whether she wanted to go or not, but she followed the Black

Knight till they came to a place where there were a lot of gravestones scattered about. At least, Alice thought they were gravestones until she read on one of them:

ON THIS SPOT (OR NEAR HERE)
GENERAL JOHNSON LOOKED FOR
FOUR-LEAVED CLOVERS
DURING THE BATTLE OF BUNKER HILL
JUNE 17, 1775

They passed many stones with similar inscriptions on them, when they came to one on which a mouse was working with a hammer and chisel.

The tablet read:

UNDER THIS TREE GENERAL WASHINGTON
DID TAKE COMMAND OF THE
AMERICAN ARMY
JULY 3, 1775

There was no tree in sight anywhere round, but there was a stump which Alice supposed might have been a tree once. The Mouse was busy carving NOT between the DID and the TAKE. He had done the N and was just finishing the O.

"That's the Channing Mouse," said the Black Knight. "He never believes anything he is told."

Just then the Mouse hit his thumb with the hammer, and turned round with a very annoyed expression on his face. When he caught sight of Alice and the Black Knight, he cried:

"What do you want here?"

"I just wanted to see," began Alice timidly, "what you are doing."

"Oh," said the Mouse in a relieved tone. "Well, I am just correcting this inscription. It is quite inaccurate. General Washington was never here. In fact, I find that he was never within twenty miles of here. I have also discovered that he never took command of the American Army for the simple reason that the American Army is a myth. I am now beginning to doubt that there was ever such a person as George Washington."

"There's a George Washington Cram," said the Black Knight.

"That is also a myth," said the Channing Mouse, "and I can prove it."

"Oh!" cried Alice, who had been reading another tablet, "did Paul Revere ride by here?"

"Paul Revere is another myth," said the Mouse.

"He is *not*," said the Black Knight. "He was in the class of 1770, and had a C in English *A*, a B in History 2, and—"

"Your memory is simply a legend," said the Mouse, and set to work again with his chisel.

"Come on," the Black Knight said to Alice. "Are you going to the Queen's croquet party?"

"The Queen," said the Mouse, turning round again, "is a complete fabrication. There never was such a person."

As Alice and the Black Knight walked away, Alice asked:

"Doesn't he believe in anything?"

"Nothing but himself," replied the Black Knight.

Chapter V

TWEEDLE AND TWADDLE

They were standing under a tree, each with his hand over the other's mouth. At first Alice had some difficulty in telling them apart, they were dressed so exactly alike, but she soon noticed that one of them had a very sad expression.

"That must be Twaddle," she thought. "I have heard somewhere that he has a gloomy disposition. I wonder if they can tell me the way out of the wood."

"Please—" she began aloud.

"Don't say that," cried both the little men together, uncovering each other's mouth; "it isn't literary."

"I'm not trying to be literary," Alice said.

"But you *should* try," said Twaddle, "especially when you are in our company. You see, we are very literary."

"Yes," said Tweedle pointing to Twaddle; "*he* is so literary that he's absolutely unintelligible."

Twaddle gave a deep sigh, and two large tears rolled down his cheeks.

"What *is* the matter?" said Alice. "You must have hurt his feelings."

"Oh no," said Tweedle. "He is just taking himself seriously, that's all. He is pretty good at it, but I can do almost as well. Watch me."

Thereupon Tweedle also heaved a deep sigh and two large tears trickled down *his* cheeks. This made Alice feel very uncomfortable. She thought she ought to say something to cheer them up, but was not quite certain how to begin.

"Can you tell me," she asked at last, "the way out of the wood?"

Twaddle dried his eyes with a large yellow pocket-handkerchief.

"I don't know how to *go* out," he said, "but I can tell you how to *come* out. I come out every month. That's why I am sometimes called the *Monthly*."

"And I come out every other week," said Tweedle.

"Are you coming out this week?" asked Alice.

"No. I come out last week and next week, but never this week," said Tweedle.

"But you must come out this week sometimes," Alice said.

"No, I don't," replied Tweedle. "I come out every *other* week. This week isn't any *other* week."

"How dreadfully confusing," said Alice.

"I knew he would confuse you," said Twaddle. "He's almost as unintelligible as I am. That's one reason why he is sometimes called an *Advocate*."

"Are advocates confusing?" asked Alice.

"You wouldn't ask that," said Twaddle, shaking his head sadly, "if you had ever been to law."

"Have *you* ever been to law?" Alice asked.

"Not exactly," said Twaddle, "but if we combine as they want us to, there is sure to be trouble."

"A combination in restraint of trade, you see," Tweedle explained.

"But it would be a great advantage to you," said Alice, "to join hands instead of covering each other's mouth."

"Exactly," said Twaddle, "the law and the profits."

Alice could not see that this last remark made any sense at all, but she said nothing.

"Would you like to hear some poetry?" Tweedle said after a pause.

"Not if it's very long," said Alice.

Tweedle paid no attention to her, but cleared his throat and began in a very solemn voice:

"The Taussig and the Bushnell Hart
Were lecturing in Greek.
They wept like anything to see
The benches bare and bleak.

'If these were only occupied,'
They said, 'why, we would speak.'

'If seven grinds with seven heads
Sat here for half a year,
Do you suppose,' the Taussig said,
'That we could make it clear?'
'I doubt it,' said the Bushnell Hart,
And shed a bitter tear.

'O Students, come and listen now,'
The Taussig did beseech,
'Political Economy

Is what I strive to teach,
The Bushnell Hart will also make
An unimpassioned speech.'

The Senior Student looked at him,
But never a word he said;
The Senior Student winked his eye,
And shook his wise old head—
Meaning to say that when he *slept*

He liked to have a bed.
But younger Students hurried up,
And even took the pains
To bring their note-books and their pens
For intellectual gains.
And this was odd, because, you know,
They hadn't any brains.

'The time has come,' the Taussig said,
'To lecture by and large
Upon the unearned increment

Of Cleopatra's Barge,
And what the scale of prices is
When buying stocks on marge.'

'And I,' the Bushnell Hart began,
'Will speak of many things:
First, whether slaves were really slaves,

Or whether they wore rings;
Or whether John Brown's Body
Has started sprouting wings.'

'A diagram,' the Taussig said,
'Perhaps will tell you more
Of what I mean in heading G,
Sub-heading number four.'
The Students all were silent
Excepting for a snore.

The Taussig and the Bushnell Hart
Talked on an hour or so,
Elucidating simple facts
That Students ought to know.
(The two back rows were fast asleep;
The rest were feeling low.)

'O Students,' said the Bushnell Hart,
'What have you learned to-day?
Did you enjoy my anecdotes?'
The Students did not say;
And this was scarcely odd, because
They all had passed away."

70

"How very interesting!" said Alice after it was finished.

"Contrariwise," Twaddle remarked. "It isn't poetry. I could understand every single word of it."

Chapter VI
THE QUEEN'S CROQUET PARTY

Alice walked on until she came to a very curious-looking gateway made of red bricks. Through it she could just catch a glimpse of some buildings which looked like the pictures she had seen of prisons, and a few tall poles which she thought might be gallows. While she was standing in front of the gateway trying to make out what was written over it, the White Rabbit came hurrying up.

"Come," said the White Rabbit, "get out of my way, or I shall be late for the Queen's croquet party."

"Oh!" cried Alice, "may I go with you?"

The White Rabbit looked at her in surprise.

"Of course you may come if you *want* to," he said.

"Don't I have to have an invitation card?" asked Alice.

"You have to go if you have one," the White Rabbit replied. "But otherwise you can do as you please. Come on."

Alice was very fond of croquet, and as the White Rabbit seemed to expect her to go with him, she followed him through the gate. When they were in the grounds Alice saw that what she had thought were gallows were really trees with their tops sawed off.

"What have they done to the poor trees?" she cried in amazement.

"Those are the famous Harvard elms," replied the White Rabbit. "The Queen lost her temper with them the other day, and ordered their heads cut off, which accounts for their strange appearance."

"What a terrible person the Queen must be," said Alice. "Oh! and what are those?" she cried, pointing to the prison-like buildings.

"They are the Senior Dormitories," the White Rabbit replied.

"I suppose they are called that because they are older than any others," said Alice. Then a new idea struck her. "I met a dormouse to-day," she said. "Do dormice live in dormitories?"

"Rats and mice of all kinds live in *these* dormitories, they are so old," said the White Rabbit, shaking his head sadly. "But they serve to unite the Class."

"Is the Class so very far apart?" asked Alice.

"Only one yard now," replied the White Rabbit, "but it used to be miles and miles. Wait till you see Conant and Perkins."

Alice was so puzzled by this remark that she was just about to ask the White Rabbit to explain, when she saw a large procession approaching. It was headed by the King and Queen, and after them came the Black Knight and a whole troop of other people whom Alice thought must be courtiers. When the procession came near, the Queen stepped out and looked fiercely at Alice.

"Do you play croquet?" she asked in a harsh voice.

"A little," said Alice; "that is,—"

"You've been cutting," roared the Queen, stamping her foot. "Off with her head!"

"Not yet! Not yet! your Majesty," said the Black Knight. "You forget we haven't begun the game yet."

"Take your places!" shouted the Queen.

Instantly everyone began to rush about in wild confusion. Alice soon found herself with a large fountain-pen for a mallet in her hand, standing in front of a hoop which was evidently meant to be a wicket, though it didn't seem to have any connection with the rest of the hoops which were scattered all over the grass with no attempt at order. As for the ball, it was nowhere to be seen, and Alice was wondering what she ought to do, when the King came up to her with a notebook in his hand.

"Have you gone through this wicket?" he asked.

"No," Alice replied; "I can't find any ball. Won't you please tell me what to do?"

"You have been cutting a little too much lately," remarked the King apologetically. "You ought to stop. That's all. Good morning."

"He must be the Recorder," Alice said to herself as he trotted away. "I suppose the Queen will be here soon and have my head cut off if I don't begin to play."

The game was now at its height, and the Queen was rushing about ordering executions right and left.

"Oh dear! Oh dear!" Alice heard the White Rabbit muttering as he hurried by her on his way to the next wicket. "I almost wish she *would* take my head off. After that party last night—oh dear! oh dear!"

Just then Alice looked up and saw the Queen standing in front of her.

"What are you doing?" said the Queen in a terrible voice.

"Nothing, your Majesty," Alice began timidly.

"Off with his head!" roared the Queen, pointing to her.

"But it's not a *he*," cried the Black Knight, hurrying up. "It's a *she*."

"It can't be a *she*," replied the Queen. "This isn't Radcliffe. Off with his head!"

"What is the matter, my dear?" said the King, as he ran up very much out of breath.

"Matter enough!" cried the Queen, pointing to Alice. "They say I can't take off his head because it's not a *he* but a *she*."

"Well," said the King very seriously, "if it's a *she*, of course you can't take off *his* head. However, let's see what I can do about it."

Hereupon he took from his pocket a large ball of red tape and began to wind it around Alice. He was so clumsy about it, however, that he managed to get first himself all tangled up in it, and then the Queen, without getting Alice in it at all. The Queen did her best to get out, but only succeeded in getting more wound up in it than ever, and finally stood there roaring, "Off with his head!" at the top of her lungs. It was such a funny sight that Alice could hardly keep from bursting out laughing. At last the King and Queen stopped struggling and both looked at Alice severely.

"Don't stand there like an idiot," said the King, very much out of breath. "Do something sensible."

"Recite 'You are old, Father William,' if you can," remarked the Queen.

Alice drew a long breath and began:

"'You are old, Widow Nolen,'
the young man said,
'Yet your mind is as keen as a knife;
With facts and with figures you've filled up my
head.
Should you do it at your time of life?'

'In my youth,' said the sage,
as he stopped for a drink,
'I was dull as an elderly cow;
And repeated each course so often, I think
That I ought to remember them now.'

'You are old,' said the youth,
'and you doubtless are rich.
I suppose you can do as you please;

But is it because of a miserly itch
That you charge such exorbitant fees?'

'I have answered one question,'
said Nolen. 'Now come,
You owe me three dollars or more;
I don't answer questions for less than that sum.
Be off, or I'll raise it to four.'"

"Oh dear," said Alice after she had finished, "it doesn't seem quite right somehow."

"It is wrong from beginning to end," remarked the King.

"Even if I can't have your head off," said the Queen, "I shall put you on probation for reciting such nonsense."

"Don't be ridiculous," said Alice. She was feeling quite bold, as the Queen was helpless in the net of red tape. As she walked away she heard the Black Knight say:

"Well, that's the first I ever saw the red tape *save* anyone."

Chapter VII
Alice and the White Knight

Alice wandered on through the Yard, gazing with delight at the groups of old ladies walking in the paths and admiring the buildings.

"The dear little things!" she cried, "I wonder if I could come near enough to them to catch one."

"You mustn't touch them," said a voice. "They are probably all related to me. I have so *many* relations around Boston."

Alice turned and saw a very pleasant-looking person in white tin armor seated on a wooden hobby horse. He was smiling in such a friendly fashion that Alice instantly felt a great liking for him.

"It's the White Knight, of course," she said to herself. "What a strange horse!" she continued aloud. "Can it move?"

The White Knight looked a little offended at her remark.

"It's a very *nice* horse," he said. "It's one of my hobbies. I have three or four others, but I almost always ride this one."

"What is its name?" asked Alice.

"Reform of the Elective System," said the White Knight. "It's my own invention."

"What do you call it for short?" Alice asked.

"I haven't called it that for long yet," replied the White Knight. "You don't consider three years long, do you? By the way, what do you think of my Freshman Dormitory?" he said, pointing to a square box which was hanging, with a great many other things, such as garden tools and bunches of asparagus, to his saddle. "You see I made it without any opening to keep the Freshmen together, and also so they can't get out at night."

84

"But if it has no opening, how are you going to get them in?" said Alice.

The Knight's face fell.

"I never thought of that," he said sadly. "But after all this is only an architect's model. It hasn't actually been built yet."

"Oh, then you can easily change it," said Alice.

"It hasn't been built yet," the White Knight went on without paying any attention to her, "and I don't believe it ever *was* built or ever *will* be built, but it's my own invention."

He seemed so very sorrowful about it that Alice thought she had better not say anything more, and they went on for some time in silence.

"I don't suppose you have any red tape with you," the White Knight remarked at last.

"No," said Alice, "but the Queen and the Recorder have some. I saw them with it."

"Ah, they find it very useful," the White Knight said. "Do you know what I want it for?"

"I haven't the least idea why *anybody* should want it," Alice replied.

"Well, you see my little collection," said the White Knight, pointing to his saddle. "I want to divide them up better. I have done something in that way already, but I used up all my red tape. I call it the Group System. It's my own invention."

"Oh, you want to tie them up in little bundles!" cried Alice.

"Exactly," replied the White Knight. "Now, you see, here are a rake and a hammer tied together. I call them History and Literature. That makes a Group. It's all my own invention."

"But supposing somebody wanted History and Botany instead," Alice remarked.

"He couldn't have it," said the White Knight. "They don't go together well."

"It's all very puzzling, I'm sure," said Alice.

"That's the best part of it," the White Knight replied. "But now I'm afraid I must leave you. You see, I have to go to five committee meetings, make three speeches and lay a few corner-stones before dark."

"How *do* you get time to invent so many things?" asked Alice.

"An ounce of invention is worth a pound of cure, you know," replied the White Knight. "But let me recite you some poetry about it."

"I don't like *all* poetry," Alice said.

"But you will like *this*," said the White Knight. "It's my own invention."

He then began in a sing-song voice:

> *"I'll tell thee everything I can*
> *In sober mood and tense.*
> *I saw a little Eli man*
> *A-sitting on a fence.*
> *'Who are you, little man?' I said,*
> *'And how do you come here?'*
> *And his answer trickled through my head,*
> *Escaping by one ear.*

> *He said, 'I tap for Skull and Bones*
> *Beneath the Campus trees,*
> *And beat my head against the stones*
> *When they all go to Keys;*
> *But Owen Johnson's spoiled our fun,*
> *Our tombs are dark and cold;*

And Sophomores from us do run,
And won't do what they're told.'

But I was thinking of a scheme
To make all Students work
By putting over them, as Dean,
An energetic Turk.

So, having missed what he had said,
With a forbidding frown,
I hit him gently on the head,
And shook him up and down.

He said, 'I sit upon this fence,
A Y upon my chest.
A frat-pin costing fifty cents
Adorns my fancy vest.
I've played upon the Football team,
I've rowed upon the Crew,
Phi Beta Kappa is my dream,
(Albeit somewhat new.)

'Religion, Football and the News—
I heeled them—not for fun,

Nor yet because I held the views
That such things should be done.
In College Life I did not fail,'
He cried in stalwart tones,
'Because I worked for dear old Yale,
And good old Skull and Bones.'

I heard him then, for I had done
Forming a plan for morn
Of building a Dormitory on
An island near Cape Horn.
I thanked him for his kindly speech.
It cheered me up a lot,
For, although we may fail to teach,
A Bones we have not *got.*

And now, if e'er by chance I see
Fair Harvard in the soup,
Or men of promise fail with E
Because they took a Group,
Or when I see all *Students fail,*
Or, what is worse, get locked in jail,
Or the Dean arrested without bail,
Or Sever sold at a bankrupt sale,

Or when the Gold Coast makes me quail,
Or the Social System turns me pale,
I laugh, and say in thankful tones,
'Though troubles weigh on me like stones,
At least, here *is no Skull and Bones.'"*

"How very pretty!" said Alice, after he had finished. "I enjoyed it very much."

"Good-bye," said the White Knight. "You go through that arched gateway and the whole world is before you. I have said the same thing before in Bacteriological Sermons."

"You mean Baccalaureate, don't you?" asked Alice.

"It makes no difference what I mean," the White Knight said. "But the germs of truth must be there."

"Good-bye," said Alice. "Do you know you are *quite* the nicest person I have met in Cambridge."

"It's worth while being a White Knight just to hear you say that," the White Knight answered as he turned his horse about and slowly rode away. Alice watched his strange figure from

the gateway as he went riding over the grass in the twilight. Long years afterwards, of all the people she saw in her visit to Cambridge, she remembered this one as having impressed her most. Just before he disappeared from view he turned round and waved his hand.

"Good-bye," cried Alice. "I hope sometime soon I can come again."

Visit us at
www.historypress.net